Count the Cats in Zanzibar

Count the Cats in Zanzibar

JIM CRAWFORD

Distributed by
TIDEWATER PUBLISHERS Cambridge, Maryland
1975

Copyright © 1975 by James W. Crawford

All Rights Reserved

No part of this book may be used or reproduced in any manner whatsoever without written permission except in the case of brief quotations embodied in critical articles and reviews. For information address Tidewater Publishers, Cambridge, Maryland 21613

Library of Congress Cataloging in Publication Data

Crawford, James W 1924-
   Count the cats in Zanzibar.

   1. Crawford, James W., 1924- 2. Sailing.
3. Sailboat racing. I. Title.
GV812.5.C72A33 797.1'24'0924 [B] 75-38934
ISBN 0-87033-216-3

Printed and Bound in the United States of America

Contents

Dedication vi
Acknowledgements vii
Preface ix

Neptune's Anger 1
Some Thoughts On Single-Handing 19
North Atlantic Sleighride 51
Sinbad's Table 67
The Cutter Yacht *Angantyr* 77

This book is dedicated to the memory of

Edward Everson Bishop

and

Lillian Huntington Bishop

Acknowledgements

My thanks and gratitude are unequivocally universal.
"Ask not for whom the bell tolls...."

Formal thanks are due to the Editors of "Motor Boating," "Skipper," "Rudder," "The South African Yachting News," and "Yachting," in whose pages these articles first appeared in a slightly different form.

Especial thanks to my friend and neighbor, Eloise Crain, for her help in typing.

The man who bent the twig and started me toward whatever success I may have had as a sailor was the late Edward Everson Bishop. Two who have had great influence on a generation of seamen and who have been unfailing examples of seamanlike behavior are my friends Irving Johnson and Rod Stephens.

My greatest debt is to the skippers and crew of the vessels in which I have sailed.

My first ship from photographic evidence was named *Chiquita*, then *Ripple, Carita, Darlin, Aleta* and *Lady Patty*. The U.S.S.N. K, Perry, DD883 was followed by *Bellatrix, Dirigo II, Desiree, Malabar XIII, Manatuck, Erivale, Fortuna, Spray, Marlene, Ticonderoga, Belle of the West, Circe, Adonde, Hoot Mon, Sea Lion, Yankee* and *Finisterre*.

It seems appropriate here to tip my hat to my friend and fellow circumnavigator in *Good News*, John Hedden. His quiet competence has my sincere admiration.

What a grand fleet of little ships and what fine shipmates! I remember them all and many more with pleasure.

Good luck, *Alnilam*!

J.W.C.

"So and no otherwise...."

Qui Non Proficit, Deficit

These five short pieces are like yarns told in the watch below. They are flashes of reality which illuminate a tiny portion of the eternal sea.

The title is an expression of one of my firmly held beliefs—my philosophy, if you like. Thoreau said, "It is not worthwhile to go around the world to count the cats in Zanzibar."

But it *is,* shipmates, it IS—for me and for many others.

The photographs speak for themselves to those who will listen. I rather think that a thoughtful person could learn a little seamanship from them and perhaps absorb some of the peace and beauty and joy and terror of the restless sea.

Fair winds,

JIM CRAWFORD

Neptune's Anger

FOUR HARD CHANCES

During a varied career at sea it has been my lot to survive four rather impressive knockdowns in small sailing vessels. This does not include a couple of swampings in racing classes and an odd broach or two when aboard an overdriven ocean racer.

The first time King Neptune rubbed my face into a little reality occurred in 1946. Ned Bishop had asked me to bring his 28' knockabout sloop *Baby* up to St. Petersburg so that he could watch the start of the St. Petersburg-Havana Race of that year. Ned had also bespoken a berth for me in Harry Bureau's lovely schooner *Bellatrix,* so it was with many pleasant anticipations that John Harris and I made sail in Manatee River after dinner on Friday night. Friday night! Well, well! That never occurred to me before! But lest we come flat aback here and start off on another yarn, let's proceed.

Baby had no power, but we made good progress downriver and out across Tampa Bay in a light southwester until a little after midnight when we anchored near Bush Key to get some sleep.

We were up and breakfasted at dawn, anxious to cover the remaining half-dozen miles, so that we could see the racing fleet at dock before they made sail.

The weather had gone definitely sour during the night, and several heavy squalls hung menacingly over the bay. Without more ado, I tucked two reefs in the mains'l, weighed anchor, set the jib, and bore off for St. Petersburg.

Pretty soon I realized I had a tiger by the tail. John had no foul-weather gear, so I asked him to stay below. Blinding rain slashed down. Lightning flashed. It was all I could do to see the cardinal points on the compass and feel the windshifts on my soaked head. It was time to jibe for the approach channel to St.

Petersburg and I decided to risk it. *Baby* had a permanent backstay to a boomkin and no runners, so theoretically all I had to do was get the main amidships, hold a turn on the mainsheet cleat, put the helm up, and hope everything held. The catch was I couldn't get that main in very flat.

It was blowing like the hammers-o'-hell and even by steering with my rump, I couldn't get that double-reefed pocket handkerchief in any further than just over the quarter.

"Damned if I don't jibe her anyway," said I to myself between gasps. I was very young then, so up went the tiller and here's what happened.

She payed off all right, like a racehorse. Then the boom lifted and swung inboard with a crash fouling the permanent backstay, and over we went—flat; spreaders in the water. If the companionway hadn't been tightly shut, we'd have lost her. In a half-minute or so I managed to overhaul the mainsheet and horse the boom down off the backstay. A seam in the mains'l then let go, which eased the situation considerably. In five minutes the main was off her and we ran in under jib alone for the yacht basin, where we docked within an hour.

The lessons learned here are patent. To begin with, I should have handled the vessel a little better, perhaps had that main down completely before the heavy squall hit, and surely no boom should be so long that it can ever hit a permanent backstay, but I should have known that this one was!

My next scar from Neptune's lash came from a considerably more memorable affair.

We were bound northward from Key West in *Lady Patty* in 1948, returning home after the Havana Race of that year. *Lady Patty* is an exceptionally able 39' Rhodes-designed ketch. There were three of us aboard—co-owner Ned, Mary, and myself.

A bit after dark our first night out of Key West, we were proceeding northward under working canvas at about four knots in a light easterly breeze. We'd had a pleasant dinner and I had the watch. My two shipmates were below turned in. I noticed heavy lightning ahead, of the sheet variety, but heard very little or no thunder.

My oilskins and seaboots were beside me at the wheel, so anticipating a squall, I quickly handed and furled the mains'l and then togged myself for heavy weather. This left us with a jib of 170 sq. ft. and a mizzen of 180 sq. ft. *Lady Patty's* main is about 360 sq. ft., so I had reduced sail by 50%—not nearly enough, as you shall hear!

We were now doing about two knots under the reduced sail and I strained every sense into the gloom in an attempt to decide what sort of unpleasantness lay ahead. Lightning continued to flicker rapidly from the approaching cloud.

I called below that there was a squall ahead and dropped in the companionway slides and closed the hatch. The ports, I thought, were all secured as it was our cool season and we seldom opened them at all.

Suddenly, without warning, between breath and breath, the wind dropped completely—vacuum-like. The sails hung limp in the lightning-flicker. Ahead I heard a roaring sound which I thought to be heavy rain. We drifted on with bare steerageway for perhaps 40 seconds.

Then Aeolus grabbed us by the trucks and simply smashed those spars down into the Gulf of Mexico. I don't exaggerate; that's what it felt like—a giant remorseless hand capsizing a toy boat. One minute we were upright and then we were over. I was up to my waist in water. Rain and spray were blown horizontally and stung like whiplashes where they hit bare skin. She was too far over to answer her helm.

The wind screamed. And from below I could hear Mary's sobbing panic-stricken screams; oddly enough, a phrase of Jack London's popped into my head, "The women screamed like stuck pigs." They do . . . a terrible sound.

For perhaps 30 seconds I concentrated on holding on. Then the jib exploded—nothing but snapping streamers left.

She was still on her beam ends, but fighting hard. I clawed my way to the mizzen halliard, about four feet (they seemed like miles!) from the wheel and let it go on the run. Nothing happened. Then, inch by inch I dragged that nearly horizontal sail down until with a snap like a grenade it also went to ribbons.

Then I felt her head slowly pay off and ponderously her lee rail emerged from the sea. But how sluggishly she rolled!

To be first in anything is usually great fun. Here's the jolly crew of Malabar XIII, *a 53' Alden Ketch, pictured in Havana before the first transatlantic race to San Sebastian, Spain, after World War II.*

We were first to finish the 4,300-mile course and first on corrected time. Great fun! More fun than glory, really. There were only three other contestants: Gaucho, *a heavy cruising ketch owned by the delightful Uriburus of Argentina, and two beautiful but unsophisticated schooners,* Bellatrix *and* Sunbeam.

We were admonished in a pre-race telegram from "Cooch" Maxwell, "If you don't win—don't come back!"

Standing (left to right), Bob Cooke, Paul Palmer, Bill Powers, Horace Binney; seated (left to right), owner Kennon Jewett, Frank MacLear, J.W. Crawford, and Dick Bertram. Phil Clarke, our cheerful cook, must have been in town.

Ned came out of the companion hatch like a charging grizzly bear.

"Lot of water below!"

"Keep her dead off!" I shouted.

He took the wheel and I jumped below into knee-deep water. I was sure she had started a butt. But I was wrong. Glancing at the engine I saw the flywheel was half under water, but with a prayer I slipped the loose belt onto the emergency bilge pump that Ned and Ingham Reeves had installed so many years ago. I pushed the start button and, by a miracle, that faithful iron tops'l caught on one cylinder, then two, then three.... She ran! Ned shouted that he could see the discharging water. She was pumping. Mary grabbed a bucket and began bailing with demonic energy. As soon as there was something for her to do, her fear left her and she turned to.

In an hour we were free of water and *Lady Patty* was her buoyant self; but what a mess below!

"Where did the water come in?" I asked Ned.

"The head port," he replied. "I was half asleep when the squall hit and woke up when thrown onto the centerboard case. Water was already squirting through the keyhole of the washroom door like a firehose."

That port is oval, 9" by 5½" and I believe that if the knockdown had lasted another two minutes, I would not be writing these lines.

Nowadays I am somewhat obsessed with having ports closed when squalls are in the offing.

My last two experiences of this sort didn't take me quite so close to Davy Jones's Locker, but they were most instructive.

The next scene is Long Island Sound in the spring. Paul Hurst and I are taking *Belle of the West,* the late Bill Erwin's 46-foot PCC, north for the Bermuda Race. *Belle* is narrow, but long-legged and well ballasted. We have cleared Stepping Stones Lighthouse and are puttering along eastward in a flat calm with the main and working jib hanging limp. It's a hazy day, close and humid. Over the Connecticut shore I see some faint flickers in the haze and hear a thump or two. Thunder? I watch that area extremely carefully. Sure enough, isn't that a line of white water coming off the land? It is!

"Down all," I shout.

Then Paul, who is about as fast a foredeck man as you're likely to meet, pulls the plug on the wire reel main halliard winch with one hand and muzzles the jib with the other. I whip gaskets around the main. When that line of white water hits us, we are under bare pole. Not a rag set. And still *Belle* is flattened until the coaming of the tightly closed midships companionway is dipping in the water. She pays off and comes up in seconds, but how hard do you suppose that wind blew?

For the last scene, here is the tale of another ocean and another vessel. The *Dirigo II*, a 60-foot Alden schooner, with a draft of 8'2", 26,500 lbs. of outside ballast and a beam of 15'6", is gently slipping along the mountainous Panamanian coast on passage from the Galapagos Islands to the Panama Canal.

We've been struggling through the doldrums and have just made landfall on Cape Mariato. It is a clear starlit night. Frank Rohr is at the wheel. I am in the cockpit smoking. Hank Hinkel and Paul Hurst are below, presumably sleeping the sleep of the just. The black jungle-clad mountains loom clearly in the night. I hear a squeak from the foregaff jaws and, tossing my cigarette overboard, I slowly mount the weather ratlines. Nothing foul; nothing chafing; just squeaking jaws. I slowly search the horizon.

What is that black line there under the mountains? A little warning bell rings in my head. I descend hurriedly, grab the binoculars and peer intently toward the dark mountains. Sure enough, it's getting closer! I clear the main halliards and stand close to Frank at the wheel. No clouds . . . no lightning. But once again the giant hand is on us. This one doesn't hit with a crash, but (at a guess) the wind velocity went from 5 knots to 75 knots within 40 seconds.

"Run her off," I snap, as I feel it come. But she doesn't quite make it before she is nearly on her beam ends and the cabin house is in the water.

"What'll I do?" yells Frank three feet from where I'm holding on to a stanchion like grim death.

"Hang on!" I roar back against the wind.

And *Dirigo II*, the grandest seagoing vessel it has ever been my pleasure to command, pays off and I start for the main peak halliard.

Hank and Paul slam the companion hatch open and shut. They've obviously been waiting under it until she righted herself. I grab the wheel, struggling to hold her dead off, and Frank runs forward to join those two battling webfoots as they hand everything except the stays'l. The wind pressure is so strong on the fores'l (only 407 sq. ft.) that they have to clap on a four-part tackle to downhall the throat. Sailors, by God! Soon we're snugged down, and the dour three-day beat against a full gale to Cape Mala isn't part of this story. Someday I'd like to tell it.

We were 28 days at sea on this passage, and this photograph gives some idea of the isolation in the days before single-sideband.

It's just after dawn and I expect the watch officer is about to get the luff on the heads'l sweated up. The mizzen stays'l (off the wind workhorse) is tacked to weather and pulling like a mule.

The sea is smooth and the bow wave is talking. It's galley weather and breakfast will be welcome.

Trim the genoa! A study in concentration. Paul Palmer watches the luff, Ken Jewett the compass and horizon to see which way the bow is swinging. Bill Powers tails while Bob Cook provides the Norwegian steam.

Ocean races are won by preparation, judgment, endurance and drive. Each sail change must be a little faster than one's competitor's. And a hungry, tense crew will seldom win long races. One must have a good ship, a good crew, and the indispensable ingredient, good fortune.

Horace Binney steers with care as Dick Bertram passes a knife to Frank MacLear.

Constant attention is needed to any seagoing sailing vessel's rig. The sea is a restless place and that old saw about eternal vigilance being the price of safety at sea happens to be absolutely true.

I love this photograph! It shows all the joy of being aboard a hard-driven windjammer nearing the end of a long passage.
The wind is fair and we are thundering into the Bay of Biscay.
Bob Cooke is at the wheel and Bill Powers is doubtless pleased not to be motorcycling about on the Western Desert as a RNVR naval gunnery liaison officer.

Malabar XIII *at the start of the Fastnet Race of 1951.*

We are still under the lee of Egypt Point and when we reached the open Solent the #1 jibtops'l disintegrated with a bang. These were the last days of cotton sails. Nowadays the rigs usually fail first.

Later, off the Needles, a lower shroud turnbuckle (rigging screw) failed and the mainmast went over the side. Uffa Fox, who was at the Needles Lighthouse, said he thought the wind was gusting to 60 knots.

I was forward at the time preparing to pull down another reef in the main and looking aft. I have a visual memory of the mainmast truck missing Alf Loomis by about six feet.

I've never liked bronze turnbuckles since and have specified steel on my own boats.

"MALABAR XIII" FASTNET RACE, 1951.

Some Thoughts On Single-Handing

The first two single-handers I knew were Captain Billy Hamlin of the *Phantom* and Captain Tom Annadown of the *Ina*. The *Phantom,* a yawl, and the *Ina,* a schooner, were beamy, shallow draft, gaff-headed vessels about 45 feet overall that sailed the Gulf of Mexico in fair weather and foul as trading vessels. When I knew them, in the early thirties, they brought coconuts from Cape Sable and conch shells from the Florida Keys to be sold to tourists in the then small towns of Fort Myers, Sarasota, Bradenton and St. Petersburg. When the cargoes were sold, Cap'n Tom and Cap'n Billy took sailing parties on the beautiful shallow bays of Florida.

These men were professional seamen and superb ones. They were weatherwise and jacks-of-all-trades. I remember with great pleasure calling at Boca Grande one windy March to find Captain Tom sitting on his cabin trunk sewing an entire new suit of sails by hand—his brown, muscled hands wielded needle and palm with rhythmic artistry.

Many years later in San Pedro, California, where I had sailed in my schooner, *Dirigo II,* I met an 80-year-old man named Harry Pigeon. In the 1920's Harry had built himself a 34' Seabird yawl (with no power whatsoever) he named *Islander* and sailed her around the world by himself.

And then, "to visit friends," he had done it again. On his third trip, with a wife this time (and that's a lovely story I'd like to tell), a tropical cyclone had found them in a coral lagoon. *Islander* parted from her ground tackle and was driven ashore. Harry and his bride, uninjured and undaunted, eventually got back to California and built another, smaller *Islander* which they were living aboard when I knew them.

"Harry, sir," I said, "What's it like to sail around the world?"

The ice-blue eyes twinkled at me and, quick as a flash, the answer came back. "You can sail one day, can't you, Jim? That's all it is—one day after the other." Which says a great deal, if you think about it.

The seed was planted and five years later, in 1958, we cast off and sailed our schooner *Dirigo II* around the world—mostly short-handed (sometimes very!) but never entirely alone. It was two years of "heaven, hell and salt water."

By the present decade I was growing grey and a mite creaky in the joints, but I had acquired a superb, modern cruising cutter named *Angantyr* and a beautiful and wise Swedish wife, who said, "You'll never be happy until you've crossed at least one ocean single-handed."

And so I went. From Falmouth in the tight little island of England, to Funchal, Madeira, and then to Antigua in the West Indies on the other side of the Atlantic basin. We—*Angantyr*, "Brum-Brum," my mascot bear, and I—were seven days to Madeira and 20 days from Madeira to Antigua. Good passages by any standards, but then, *Angantyr* is an exceptional boat and a lucky one.

Why? Well, my friend, Tom Follet, who has done at least four single-handed transatlantics, says in *Project Cheers*, "... I can't pin down any reasons that make sense or, at least that would make sense to anyone other than myself. Certainly not 'because it's there.' I like heated rooms and feather beds, cloths of silk and shoes of fancy leather. I like wine served in good crystal, well cooked food on fine china and a fair young maid standing by telling me what a fine chap I am. I do not like the North Atlantic Ocean. You figure it out."

Bravo, Tom! We'll leave the "why" of it to the shade of William Washburn Nutting, first Commodore of the Cruising Club of America, who most certainly would reply, "Why? For the hell of it, that's why!"

How? Now that puts us on steadier ground or calmer seas, if you like. And instead of telling you how to design and build the perfect single-hander (which Robert Clark can do much better than I), I'm going to yarn away on how to single-hand most anything—the boat you hopefully now have, or the dreamship in your mind's eye. Somewhat facetiously I've been replying to people who ask how I single-hand my own vessel, "When they get too big to paddle, they're all about the same." Think about that a bit. And at once let me say that I flunked Charles Atlas's course 30 years ago; by religion I'm a D.C.—Devout Coward, that is.

"Give me a lever and a place to stand," said the old Greek, "and I shall move the earth." Translate that as, "See to it that your boat is adequately winched and that you know what a purchase is." Mechanical advantage—that's one of the secrets. You know how they handled the great steel Cape Horners of yesteryear? Brace winches, that's how. They were invented by a man named Jarvis—Captain "Brace Winch" Jarvis.

And why not pamper your auxiliary engine, which I'd say is worth six salty seamen and never talks back or gets entangled with foreign "wimmen?"

Of course, on one transatlantic (of my *Angantyr's* six, as of present writing) I was fool enough to have slighted the maintenance on our iron tops'l and naturally it resented this and went *non mŏtus*. Thank heavens, there were two of us that time—good John Shannahan standing watch and watch with me, and fortunately the engine failed when we were well offshore where we are usually 100% windjammer anyway. Near the land is where reliable power cuts fatigue in half.

Did I say fatigue? Aha! The evil cat's out of the bag already. Fatigue is the troublemaker, the "Invisible Rust," as one recent article in *Naval Institute Proceedings* described it. We'll come back to this bugaboo later.

Now for two modern bits of gear which have helped the single-hander quite a bit—the electronic autopilot and the wind-vane steerer. Of these I plunk strongly for the autopilot—both are the absolute *best*.

Caveat emptor on autopilots, indeed *all* gear which you intend to take to sea. When all else fails, read the specifications before you buy and the directions after. Each of these—the wind vane and the autopilot—can be worth two men.

The wind for the wind vane is free and the autopilot consumes electricity, not roast beef and beer. Neither of these gadgets gets tired. They do wear out, however, so as for spares, carry two or three of everything.

Which brings us back to our old enemy—fatigue.

"Fatigue", says an old Capetown sailor friend, Frank Robb, "is a spell cast over the human mind and body by three wicked witches of the Lack family. They work together and their names are: Lack of Food, Lack of Comfort, and Lack of Sleep."

Food requirements are quite individual. Some people do well on very little (but well selected) food. At the other extreme, I eat five times a day (all rather light meals) even ashore. At sea, I keep raisins and nuts handy and love the bubbling sound of the old teakettle. I'm also an aficionado of Ovaltine and cocoa in dreary weather. Mug up before you give up, is my motto. In addition, I'm convinced that supplementary vitamins are desirable for maximum efficiency.

Comfort can be equated with warmth and dryness. Get your oilskins on *before* the first dollop of spray—especially the trousers. There's nothing more disenchanting than a wet fanny. And if you do your sailing with the bark on in the colder half of the year, copy the people who work out there *all* year 'round . . . wear hip boots.

See to it that as little water as possible gets below by having tight decks and adequate non-watergulping ventilators. The *Dorade* ventilator was the first well known one, and there are several modern variations.

In the sunny middle parts of the earth, arrange for adequate protection from the sun. Don't scorn the ubiquitous umbrella . . . the Fijians don't.

If following the whale road in Viking seas, be sure you have a good seagoing cabin stove. Whether it burns solid fuel such as wood or coal, or diesel, or even liquid petroleum gas (propane-butane) such as Chichester had in *Gypsy Moth V* is of little importance. They are all good if well installed and sensibly used. Make yourself as comfortable as you can, then when trouble comes your tail will be up, and you'll weather it.

The worst and most dangerous of the witches is lack of sleep. If you don't get about eight hours of sleep out of 24, your judgment will suffer—badly. Caution: There very well might go the ball game. Fortunately you do not need all eight hours of sleep at one time.

On one passage in the schooner *Dirigo II,* returning from the Hawaiian Islands after a Transpac, there were just three of us on board—Hank Hinkel, Wilson Cross, and myself. We stood two hours on and four off. None of us ever slept the entire four, but we and our ship arrived in San Luis Obispo in better shape than we have ever been since.

On my single-handed transatlantic I never slept more than three consecutive hours and often—say near Finisterre where shipping lanes are heavily traveled—I kept a kitchen timer set for 15-minute intervals between look-sees. (A timer should be bought with the autopilot.) One *must* sleep. "Sleep that knits the ravelled sleeve of care."

Now some thoughts on the little ships themselves. If you are 19 and haven't made your first million, a very small vessel will do the job—*If you have the training and* (rather uncommon) *common sense.*

Yet on the whole I strongly recommend the largest vessel you can afford. The motion is easier (less tiring). The vessel will go faster with less driving. And you can carry some good books and fancy grub—this sort of thing is supposed to be fun.

Rig? It matters less than one might think. There are good yawls, good ketches, and good sloops (and don't discount the schooner rig). With modernization, I think we're going to see some interesting things in the next few years; take a look at the Dick Carter-designed *Vendredi,* which was single-handed across the North Atlantic in 1972.

Hull form? Ask any reputable naval architect. My own conviction, after some 40-odd years of deepwater and shoal, is that when the mighty ocean wants to come aboard, it will, whether you have a Colin Archer, Contessa, or a Catamaran. Then it's best to have a *strong* little ship under one's feet.

Finally, the apprenticeship for almost any trade is a minimum of seven years, and the trade of the seaman is still a noble art which can only be learned by study and practice.

Dirigo II *crossing the finish line of the St. Petersburg-Havana Race in 1953.*

Just a few minutes before this picture was snapped, I asked John Alden if he would like to take her across the line. Carleton Mitchell's Caribbee *was in sight ahead. "No thanks, Jim," he replied, "it's what you're payin' for."*

We were second across the line (ahead of Ticonderoga *and the M-Boat* Doris III*), second in the Fleet and second in Class A on corrected time—and first schooner!*

Olé, *as the log comments.*

She took me around the world, this lovely schooner. We once sailed 1,067 miles in five consecutive days; over 200 miles a day on the blue surface of earth's largest physical feature—the Pacific Ocean.

Here is a deck view as we close-reach through Yucatan channel bound for Panama.

The fores'l boom tackle looks snug, but perhaps we should secure the weather tops'l sheet with rotten stopping to keep it from chafing.

Dirigo II *was built for Charles Van Sicklen who rounded Cape Horn in* Wanderbird.

She had fore- and maintopmasts with white doublings and I gold-leafed her lofty trucks.

She was a sailing machine for going to faraway places and looking just right when she got there.

A view from the end of Dirigo II's *18-foot bowsprit as she dives into the bright Caribbean.*

If there is anything more beautiful than a windjammer on a sparkling tradewind day, I haven't seen it.

Doldrums! Now here's a contrast! Stark calm on the lap of the line.
We are becalmed at passage to the Galapagos and Paul Hurst is transferring fuel into the tanks.
Frank Rohr's face is obscured by the boom tackle, but I hope he looks up once in a while for waterspouts form rapidly in this area.

Wilson Cross glasses Margarita Island on the Mexican Coast. Predictably, the pair of peaks are called Las Tetas.
Note the heavy foreboom bail, the spray hoods on the hatches and the not-too-neatly-lashed turnbuckle covers. I trust the turnbuckle threads are well greased.

Hank Hinkel, seaman, seacook, yachtbroker, and a fellow rascal in Paradise (old Tahiti hand) poses with the biggest dolphin I've ever seen.

We were at passage from the Galapagos toward Panama when this big fellow bit on a bone tuna lure and bent the hook.

Wilson Cross once gazed upon a similar bull-headed dolphin and remarked softly, "Looks just like my father." Now, shipmates, find a picture of Wilson elsewhere in this spread and maybe you can imagine why he said that.

Dolphins, even those as large as this one, are delicious eating. They are sold as Mahi-Mahi at the Royal Hawaiian and would grace any royal table.

They are truly offshore fish and are found wherever flying fish sparkle in the sunlight.

Leviathan comes calling. Whales are an awesome sight at sea. They have an occasional habit of sinking small ships—yesteryear, large ones, too, when whalers were built of wood. The whaleship Globe *was disastrously dealt with by an enraged sperm whale in the 19th century.*

This curious fellow came over the horizon in a flat spot in the North Pacific and scared hell out of us. Hank Hinkel was on watch and Wilson Cross and I sought emotional safety aloft with our cameras. The monstrous visitor (he was about as long as the ship) dove right under us athwartship giving us a proper fright and then followed in our wake puffing periodically for a considerable time, with Hank glancing nervously astern. After a bit, he remembered an appointment and steamed off.

Question: Was he or she bent on matrimony?

Tagus Cove, Isla Isabela, Galapagos; Las Islas Encantadas of the first explorers.

The cool Humboldt Current and volcanic topography make these very strange islands indeed. Magnetic anomalies, unpredictable currents, and occasional fog make for nervous navigation.

When one rows ashore here, seals play within inches of the oar swirls and descendants of the finches that so interested Darwin remain perched close by.

Becalmed in the North Pacific High.

About a thousand miles north of the Hawaiian Islands is just about as far from terra firma as one can get.

This photograph was taken from an inflatable raft and it was so silent here in the vast Pacific that an echo would be returned from the sails.

In the long and gentle swell the hull will drop from sight in a few seconds.

Details aloft showing the parrel beads instead of mast hoops, the fidded topmasts, and wooden gaff jaws.

Dirigo II's rig was pure "Wanderbird" and her hull was pure Alden.

Ben Tindall-Pooley taps out a message to a fellow amateur radio operator.

Amateur radio, and particularly CW (code), is just about the cheapest and best communication for the world-ranging vessel.

Modern single-sideband is effective and very expensive. I would rather have Ben aboard, who never had any trouble raising the States from the middle of the Coral Sea.

Here we are moored off the Botanical Gardens, Brisbane, Australia.
Kookaburras squawk at dawn and we wander through the fruit-laden markets with delight after a year in the tropics. Bananas and coconuts are romantic, but not as nourishing as apples and plums.

"The anchor is weighed and the sails they are set . . . ," as the old chantey goes.

We're leaving St. Helena in the South Atlantic under four lowers. The little town is St. James and we were given a quarter of a lamb here by Mr. Tucker whose father had done the same for Slocum of the Spray. The photograph is by Anthony Cross, A.D.C. to the Governor.

North Atlantic Sleighride

At noon on June 11, 1955, seven racers crossed the starting line at Brenton's Reef Lightship, off Newport, Rhode Island, bound for Marstrand in Sweden. They were *Carina, Circe, Ortac, Peter von Danzig, Stavanger, Kormoran,* and *Schlussel von Bremen*—four West German, two American, and one Swedish.

I had the good fortune to be navigator aboard *Circe*—a Sparkman and Stevens designed beauty (56 ft. L.O.A.; 39 ft. L.W.L.; 11 ft., 9 in. beam, and 8 ft. draft) owned by Carl Hovgard of New York.

Following is my diary written in brief snatches as we battled through the gales and calms of the North Atlantic. I haven't attempted to dress it up; this is the way it is. Come aboard!

1640, June 11, 1955:

No Man's Land is fast disappearing on the port quarter. A dreary sight in the misty rain, Vessel going well, 8½ knots, and that's the last of land we should see until North Ronaldsay in the Orkneys. A miserable misty day for a start and all of us quite tense—"real shook," as Danny puts it. I think we were first across the line at that but without much way on—nevertheless, a good start.

Carina close aboard to weather, but she couldn't hold us although she was a little quicker with her mizzen stays'l. Finally she went under us and disappeared on course of Vineyard Sound.

We elected to go outside, as did *Kormoran* and another unidentified vessel. I think it the correct decision.

2215, June 11:

It's not so murderously cold now. Breeze has eased. Still overcast. Don't like *Kormoran* holding us so well—she just crossed about one-half mile astern of us. Sankaty Head is on the port beam flashing farewell.

Had a fine dinner: ham, potatoes and string beans.

Every time I sail in someone else's boat I compare her to *Dirigo II*. Inevitably and humanly it's an unfavourable comparison for the other boat! But one certainly does learn a lot from other boats. So far here I am most impressed by the coffee grinder and the deadlights. Was aboard *Stavanger* for a few moments this morning, and her heavy gear certainly reminded me of

Dirigo. For ocean passages I'd say that one pays a little too much for the windward ability of vessels of *Circe's* sort.

Am writing by flashlight—Bud is snoring stentoriously below me.

1140, June 12:

Cold, raining, blowing, miserable! But going wonderfully. This morning we rang the changes from large genoa to small and then to working jib. I ran her off each time and all went well. Ralph a little green, but expect he will pick up in a day or two. We are now close reaching on starboard tack at nine knots and quite comfortable, all considered.

Have come below and dried off thoroughly and changed. Think we should crack 200 today, but haven't seen the sun yet; so expect we'll only have a D.R. noon position.

She filled her cockpit pretty thoroughly before we shortened down. If she starts those tricks again, we'll single reef the main. May not be necessary.

How Dick and Paco would love this kind of going! It would certainly be nice to have them here.

1714, June 12:

Still thundering along—still raining, still cold—shifted back to large genoa an hour or so ago.

Just been experimenting with soapstone fireplace—have a nice little fire going. Hope it behaves. Various chores: Head canvas, time zone chart, weather time schedule, and an hour wheel trick have kept me pretty busy. Must get a little sack time before supper.

2108, June 12:

Grand turkey dinner by Bud under comparatively difficult conditions. My stove experiments have borne fruit. The cabin is considerably warmer. Wind still well forward of the beam—just laying course with cracked sheets—and the old gal has the bit in her teeth.

1535, June 13:

Night of the 12-13th was wild, wet, windy and very thick with fog. By dawn, however, we had the mizzen stays'l and large light genoa on her, and the motion somewhat improved. Hellacious leftover sea without a great deal of wind in the sleazy hours before dawn. Morning continued to improve—ran out of the fog at 1015 and it has been lovely ever since. 9 M. sun lines and local apparent noon sight.

2245, June 13:

Just got the engine going for battery-charging purposes after a six-hour struggle. Danny did the struggling, not I. Had forgotten to secure gate valve until an hour after start, and this is the penalty. Fumes and working in the believe-it-or-not heat put me off my feed. Better now.

1745, June 14:

Ship's clocks have been set ahead one hour. All hell has busted loose with the spinnakers. Three sail failures since dawn, when we set the first chute.

And the ship's conversation has grown venereal—all symptoms of longhaul ocean racing in small ships. Bud's chow ("when you're at Hall's you're at home") continues good. It is great to be warm once again. Am now in khaki shirt and trousers instead of woolen shirt, thermowear, and oilskins.

Dan went aloft this noon to pull down a spinnaker halliard. I steered and attempted to keep her steadied down as much as possible.

1820, June 14:
Bob has a rumba going on shortwave from Merrie England. I am skimming *Time*. Caught this: Samuel Eliot Morison, "and when you go out on the tide, don't bother with the channel. Go out between the two little islands. It's narrow, and there's a big rock in the middle and it will scare hell out of you. But it's beautiful." Bud: "Sven, Derek wants to know how to say, 'I love you, but I don't want to marry you.'"

2230, June 14:
Just came below from a singing and joke-telling session in the cockpit. Danny working on the spinnaker on the cabin table—damn sewing machine acting up. I predict—Dan'l will fix it.

1020, June 15:
Dan'l fixed it.

2000, June 15:
We are undergoing a very reasonable imitation of a Western Ocean summer gale. Heavy westerly squalls. Dan damn near got himself hurt while winging out the small genoa as a running sail. Lift was let go on the run; tip of pole went in the water pinning Dan against the swifters.

1640, June 16:
Summer gale eased by dawn but nasty seaway remained. First water tank went dry. Bud uses an amazing amount of water. Wish Hank were along. Busy this morning with 9 M. star lines, a.m. sun lines, noon sight, etc. Thickening up this p.m.—and haven't had p.m. sun lines. Derek has a bottle with "*Circe* was here" on it for Point "A."

Just now we storm along with a very easy motion—board reaching on starboard tack. Had a nice alcohol bath today. Derek bathed overboard. B-r-r-r. Dan tells story of the "war" they put on for the visitor to the Korean front from Washington.

Dan just by my bunk for a lesson on Nautical Almanac.

0805, June 17:
Bud: "There's this steward that stutters; he comes running up to the Captain, "C-c-c-captain, the-the-the . . ." "Well, for God's sake, man, if you can't say it, sing it."

"Sh-she-should o-old acquaintance be forgot and never brought to mind . . . the cook's fell overboard and is f-f-fifteen miles behind."

A wild, wild, tobogganing night easing at a foggy dawn with porpoises. Now very light. Many stories with breakfast. Bud and Bob in high form. Variation on moose story.

1820, June 17:
Bull session in cabin. Self, Carl, Dan—Bob copying code. Breezing on from East; just faired so can lay course. Dan a wrestler in school. Coal fire just fine below. Smells good.

1300, June 18:
Radio playing "The Bells of San Raquel." Bud dancing in galley. Salmon and peas for dinner. Cold clear blue on deck. A good drying day. Ralph and I took sun line.

2110, June 18:
Herming up for a gale. Breezed on hard. Falling barometer, cloudy, high sunset—"making up for no good," says Dan, who is now in foc'sl repairing head of spinnaker which let go a couple of hours ago. This is the sort of thing one views with equanimity—from a *Stavanger* or *Dirigo II*, but with some trepidation from a highly tuned violin such as *Circe*. Must to sleep to rest up for???

1805, June 19:
We seem to have weathered that one with only three gear failures: The spinnaker head mentioned before, the luff wire on the mizzen stays'l, and a halliard shackle deformed.

We now recall many gale warnings. The Mother Carey's chickens called all night, one even came aboard. We saw the traditional high cirrus bands. A high sunset. Bud's neck hurt. And last but not least, the barometer fell. The barograph seems to be by far the more sensitive instrument.

It's now colder than a witch's tit (Bob) and Carl is building a fire in the soapstone fireplace meanwhile joshing me about my defeat by the fireplace a couple of nights ago.

Bud is stirring about in the galley—producing good smells and vaudeville routines.

Carl: "The most important thing about lighting this fire is to light it and then walk nonchalantly away; that scares the hell out of it."

0025, June 20:
Standing Dan's watch tonight while he mends spinnaker (which he's just finished) and mizzen stays'l. Beautiful, cold night. Still some light of an odd sort in the west at midnight. Saw basking sharks at dusk. Fins four feet high!

1710, June 20:
Just thought of a title for the forthcoming masterpiece as the wind came in from N.W. after a.m. calm . . . "Reach for North Ronaldsay."

2015, June 20:
Ike talking on radio, nobody paying much attention. Such things seem very far away and relatively unimportant.

Passed through a considerable school of "muldoan" sharks at suppertime —some within a few feet. Sea monsters, indeed. Beautiful sunset, birdlife growing more numerous.

0010, June 21:
Just called on deck—old gal high, wide and wild. Bob handed mizzen. Eased steering. Wind very dry, hands feel dry. Barometer rising.

1108, June 22:
All of the 21st was a genuine Western Ocean summer gale. We really tore yesterday (21st) p.m. we set the working jib and small genoa as twin spinnakers—a really excellent deal.

Handed same this morning as it had gone light. Bud announced that it was "galley weather" and produced some delicious pancakes and ham. Just at end of breakfast, the cotton spinnaker let go in the centre—considerable action for a few minutes. Dan has now completely repaired the sail with Ralph assisting.

2022, June 22:
Went from very light and shifty fair wind to hard-on-the-wind port tack at suppertime. Wind breezed on, but has now eased, and all is very peaceful with started sheets.

2012, June 23:
We're really headed for the barn today—180 miles after having been pretty well becalmed yesterday. We have been reaching hard. First close-reaching and now broad-reaching.

Carl has been battling (unsuccessfully) with the fireplace. Much raucous laughter from me and Danny. Ralph a little off his feed again.

Sven (we are discussing logs and driftwood at sea): "You hit a big log right smack in the middle; (lift of Swedish eyebrows) that's bad!"

Danny at lunch was telling of his school experiences. He was quite a lad. Successfully stole the clapper from the chapel bell at Exeter. Admitted guilt after receiving diploma.

Circe strides along using every inch of her overall length. She often surfs down off the seas with spray flying like wings from either bow. Once and a while a sea catches her and gives her a good dousing. Bud, an ex-trawler cook, shipfitter, piano player, comedian. He can cook under absolutely appalling conditions and tell jokes while doing it.

2015, June 24:
Tempers a little short today. Mine, at least. Can't find (and apparently didn't bring) a chart I'd like to have. Infuriating. Definitely remember getting it in wrong pile at City Island. Ass that I am! Wind is now right aft. Stove works. Lit by me—boat going like hell. If it blows any harder, we'll have to reef. Rain squalls from astern.

Carl a little tired today: Took extra sack time in afternoon watch. I'm fit as a fiddle. Have never had it quite so easy—so far. Still very much wish MacLear or Bertram could have made it. Think then I would have insisted on having a watch. I always sleep well when one of those sea gulls is on deck.

We are growing literary. Everyone reading. Sven brought *Run Silent, Run Deep;* Ralph, *Conquest by Man;* Derek, a book on the Far East, otherwise unidentified; and I, *Fair Winds in the Far Baltic, The Breaking Wave,* and *Daniel Boone.* There are quite a few pocket books aboard. Am reading *Scaramouche* now.

1751, June 25:

Fun and games last night. Bob had just called me at 2300 to try Consol when Sven yelled that the steering gear had let go. Panic party. Went on through the night under jury gear until Dan had replaced the sheave that let go. Damn composition sheave. Steered by the emergency compass lashed on the companion slide as the repair necessitated the removal of the steering compass.

Had quite a scrap re-lashing the upper slide before re-setting the main— Derek and I. Morning brought somewhat clearer skies and sun lines, thank God!

After lunch we jibed in a damn dangerous manner. Derek and I on foredeck. Pole almost took charge. Long Island Sound spinnaker work not apropos on the Western Ocean. When the tumult and shouting subsided, I sounded off pretty sharply that the next time we jibed, I ruddy well wanted to do it. Rest of the afternoon I spent trying to start our thoroughly wet engine. Get very close, but have had to secure for supper. This motherless installation needs a good going over. Clouded over and drizzling again.

2036, June 25:

Much excitement! *Saxonia* just altered course to pass ¾ of a mile astern in the mist and rain. We must be a stirring sight driving along with the 'chute set at 10 knots.

2032, June 26:

Got charging engine going today. Some sun lines in a.m. Went south of Rockall. Quite tired. Fine dinner—with apple pie!

0123, June 28:

Today (the 27th) full of excitement. Landfall on Boreray. A trawler close aboard. Many gannets, puffins, etc. Scotch coast impressively sombre. Finished *Scaramouche* today—a good novel.

1945, June 30:

Reached under the Orkneys in calm water and some light air. Very poor visibility as usual. Quite a thrill passing North Ronaldsay. Then into a Christ-awful seaway which persists. Hard on the wind starboard tack.

2122, June 30:

The seaway persisted until dawn of the 29th but fell away rapidly then. The 29th we'd like to write off the books. The sea went down and the wind with it. Then the fog came in. Flat becalmed, or nearly so, throughout the evening and night of 29th to 30th. At dawn today I tossed a Roosevelt dime to Aeolus; surreptitiously stuck my knife in the mast; and whistled the "British Grenadiers" and "Hay en el Rancho Grande!" Naturally the wind came in.

We have been making fine progress since. Ralph shaved. I have been very busy with RDF as no sights possible. Many trawlers about. Sub passed us at dusk. Very modern looking. Sven says Swedish. All hands anxious to get in, but I try to restrain predictions—very unlucky.

1853, July 2:

We have finished and lost badly. *Carina* beat us boat-for-boat by three hours and *Kormoran* followed within a short time. Saw her stand in as we ate breakfast at the Hotel Marstrand.

I spent the last day and night on deck without sleep. As Bob put it, I wore out the companionway going from the chart table to the deck. We were becalmed badly on the first of July, so badly that Derek and I went off in the dinghy for pictures.

The finish was a heartbreaker. We finished; the committee launch came alongside and said we were the second in—*Carina* first. Deepest gloom! Damn those spinnakers!

Our spirits bounced back rapidly after a schnapps or two and a little reflection. We had sailed our vessel hard and well. After 3,450 miles, the first three vessels had finished within a period of six hours. What a wonderful race! Well done, *Carina!*

Reefing Circe, *a 55' Sparkman and Stephens yawl in the cold North Atlantic during the Newport-Marstrand Race of 1955.*

Dan Walker steers and Sven Hansen is intent on the clew of the mains'l. The heads'ls help steady her, but she will be happier with the main backup.

The view from aloft on one of the few bright days of this transatlantic race. Carl Hovgard steers as Circe *broad-reaches along at eight knots.*

Derek Wilde, Bob Erskine, and Dan Walker inspect a broken headboard slidelashing.

The ability to promptly repair minor gear failures is of paramount importance in deepwater racing. I judge we had the sail back on her in 30 minutes.

This mishap probably cost us at least two hours. "Mistakes," as Rod Stephens wrote me later, "are very costly."

Becalmed in the Skaggerak.
Circe looks lovely, but is not going anywhere very fast.

Sinbad's Table

Sailors are notorious trenchermen. Some of them, of course, are just plan notorious.

Over the course of some 40 years and many thousands of miles of sea water—hot and cold, and including once around this lovely earth—I have collected recipes. These recipes are unique. I defy you to find them in any other cookbook. If you do find them in another cookbook, please write me. The poltroon stole them from the same place I stole them and I'd like to meet him and have a yarn. He'd be an interesting fellow.

Cookbooks are usually written by women. This is a mistake; women are beautiful, desirable, and delightful creatures but they aren't logical. It takes the keen analytical male brain for cookbooks; mine. Besides males do most of the eating. Sheer proof!

At any rate, the art of cookery is an adult occupation, avocation, or what-you-will. This is adult. It assumes that you already know how to open a can of beans and boil water. Newlyweds and geriatric consumers of TV dinners can skip it.

Mood music is indicated. Make with the paso doble, with the gazpacho, and skirl the pipes with the haggis. There isn't any haggis in here, but you get the idea. *Bon appétit!*

Dick Bertram, the debonair sailing speedboat man, and Frank MacLear, the yacht designer, and I sailed my schooner *Dirigo II* in the Honolulu Race of 1953. We had a gang of good types aboard and a fine time was had by all. It's wonderful to carry a spinnaker for 12 days under a trade-wind sky.

In Honolulu we landed among friends and one of the best was Carrie Guild, who wrote *Rainbow in Tahiti*. She had us for lunch in her lovely home on Wailupe Circle and the *pièce d'occasion* was a marinated tomato dish which goes like this:

Peel and cut big ripe tomatoes in thick slices. Cut sweet (red) onions in very thin slices. Arrange layer of tomatoes, cover with layer of onions, salt, and freshly ground black pepper and scatter fresh herbs over all—basil, oregano, and a dash of parsley. Continue until dish is full and pour red wine vinegar and French olive oil over all—about half-and-half, according to your taste. I like it quite vinegary. Prepare at least 24 hours before serving so flavors blend; that is the secret. Keep in icebox, naturally, and serve chilled. It is superb.

To go with the marinated tomatoes I hope you can catch a snapper, bluefish, Florida redfish, or small tuna. Use a silver hook if necessary.

This recipe came from Camp Bang-Bang on Andros Island in the Bahamas, which was "back of beyond" in 1952 when we anchored there in *Lady Patty*. The late Coke Rathborne (about as dashing an ocean sailing type as there has been) was there with *Malahini*. He, John and Lydia Booth, and our host Hank Thorne, helped us consume a baked snapper by Chico, the Camp's talented chef.

After cleaning the fish in the usual manner (if you can't get somebody else to do it), proceed as follows:

Chop green pepper, celery, and onion quite fine, in equal amounts—½ cup of each depending on size of fish. Mix thoroughly and sauté gently in butter; lots of butter. Then add ½ teaspoon of the freshest thyme in the house and bread crumbs sufficient to stuff the fish. Turn thoroughly to mix stuffing. Stuff the fish tightly and sew or skewer it together. Bake in a moderate oven in a greased pan after first squeezing a lemon over the fish. Clean your hands with the lemon rind.

I wish Coke Rathborne could be there to regale you with stories of pigsticking in India in the days when the sons of Eli really got around.

Seviche! Ah, Seviche! Pickled fish in many forms is served throughout the world, but this one, for my palate, is the king of them all. We've met it in fishing villages in Baja, California, in platinum hotels in plush Acapulco, and in Panama's "El Rancho" where the candlelight gleams in many a pretty senorita's eyes and the pulsing Latin American music does things to a gentlemen's judgment. You have been warned.

I once served it aboard *Dirigo II* by request when we were battling it out with a 40-knot head wind while rounding Cape Mala on a memorable homeward passage from the Galapagos. It was my turn to cook and when I asked Hank Hinkel, Paul Hurst, and Frank Rohr how they wanted the tuna we had caught on our trolling line, they unanimously voted for Seviche. Here's how it's done.

Get any really fresh white-meat fish. We usually prefer those we catch ourselves, but store-bought fish is all right, provided you know a trick. When you ask your fish-market man, "Is it really fresh?" watch his hands. If they tend to close when he says "Yes, Sir," or "Ma'm" (as the case may be), it's a fair bet he's lying. Of course, a careful sniff is proof enough.

Filet the fish and skin the filets. Then dice the firm white flesh into thumbnail-sized bits and put in a bowl. Squeeze lemon or lime juice over all; about one fruit to a large handful of fish bits. The amount is not critical. Mix thoroughly and put in icebox for at least an hour. Then remove and squeeze excess juice from the fish. You will note that the fish has turned white and appears cooked. Pour off the excess juice and discard. Next, finely dice a couple of onions and tomatoes. The correct proportions here are a heaping tablespoon of diced onion and two heaping tablespoons of diced tomato per handful of fish. Vary to taste, of course.

Now add one dash of Tabasco per handful of fish for boy's Seviche, two dashes for man's Seviche, and three dashes for hero's Seviche. (These definitions are courtesy of Wilson Cross, upon whom be the peace.) Salt and black pepper lightly. Mix well and allow to stand at least another hour in the refrigerator before serving in cocktail cups on fresh lettuce. Girls—look out!

We've been cruising recently through the lush green canals of Holland in a Dutch sailing "tjalk" with the unlikely name of *Ebenhaezer*. Like George Roosevelt's famous schooner *Mistress*, she's big and black and costs me a lot of money, but she's a lot of fun.

One day when we were anchored for lunch in an offshoot of the North Sea Canal near Amsterdam, my bride Karin came forth with the following original and taste-tantalizing composition, christened "Ebenhaezer Salad."

Take ½ green pepper, one medium onion, a cup of cauliflower florets, three small carrots, half a heart of lettuce, two tomatoes and combine in salad bowl in moderate-sized bits according to your fancy. Next, open a can of small Norwegian shrimp and pour off the juice and save. Add the shrimp to the vegetables. Next, add a #2 can of drained beansprouts of the sort the Chinese use so cleverly.

Make a dressing as follows. Press two cloves of garlic into the juice you saved from the shrimp. Add 2/3 cup mayonnaise, 1/3 cup tomato catchup, two tablespoons Worcestershire sauce, and three drops Tabasco. Lightly salt and pepper to taste.

Add the dressing to the salad and mix thoroughly. Garnish with sliced hardboiled egg and (here's the twist!), thinly sliced banana. Ambrosia!

The lordly Keeps of Spain are full of interest for those with the wanderlust. How well I remember standing with Alan Carlisle, that gay, versatile ocean wanderer, in the arabesqued interior of the Alhambra in High Granada and thinking some long, long thoughts, for in the room where we stood a lot began one day long ago. Christopher Columbus knelt there before Her Most Gracious Majesty Isabella and petitioned for a fleet to sail westward beyond the ocean's rim.

We were sailing in Alan's graceful cutter *Erivale* and bound westward, too, like our famous predecessor.

We hold much in common, Alan and I, and one of the things is an admiration for gazpacho—that supremely refreshing cold soup of Spain. Ilene Stuart, one of Madrid's most gracious hostesses, taught me how to make it. This is right for about five, so vary the amounts in proportions to suit your needs.

Take one pound white bread (three slices equal ¼ pound), ½ pound tomatoes, one large onion, two cloves garlic, one cucumber, three tablespoons olive oil, 1½ cups water, two tablespoons vinegar, and one green pepper. Soak the bread in water for two hours and when soft, break up and put in mortar with tomatoes, onion, garlic, and cucumber. Mash all well. Put through a colander and beat thoroughly; add vinegar and continue beating. Set aside in refrigerator for one hour. Then dilute with water to the consistency of very thin cream. Garnish with finely chopped cucumber and green pepper. Salt lightly to taste. Serve very cold. *Olé compañeros!*

We were snugly moored in little Aebeltoft on the east coast of Denmark when I first heard of Bana Calda. Gould and Lucia Eddy were cruising with the incomparable Irving and Exy Johnson aboard the ketch *Yankee*. I had joined her in Kiel and was relieved to get away from the hotels in which I had been temporarily quartering. We were at peace with the world in *Yankee's* great cabin after a delectable dinner by Exy.

The talk ranged from the Solomon Islands to the North Cape. Irving even mused about his projected voyage up the Nile. Somehow we sailed in reminiscence to Italy and Lucia told us of Bana Calda. It comes from around Milan.

First, you invite all your best friends. This is a grand meal for a party.

The afternoon of the big evening, hie yourself to your best source of fresh vegetables and buy heavily of just about everything you can lay your hands on. Everything must be fresh, young and tender.

Get several cabbages, red and green. Select radishes, celery, carrots, green peppers, tomatoes, cauliflowers, asparagus, cucumbers, and anything else that appeals to you and is crisp and crunchy. Carefully clean the lot and pare into attractive grabbable two- or three-bite-sized pieces. Put each ingredient on a separate dish or arrange on plates as you like. Chill them in the refrigerator all afternoon.

When the mob arrives, break out an electric frying pan, hot plate, hibachi, or what-have-you. Put it in the middle of the room. Place on it a heavy frying pan (assuming it isn't the electrified type, obviously). In the pan put four ounces of butter and four ounces of best olive oil, a couple of tins of anchovies, and a tablespoon of chopped garlic. Sauté gently. Smell that mouth-watering aroma?

The chilled vegetables have now been placed around strategically. Everybody ready? Go! The technique is take what you like with your fingers and dip into the pan. I guarantee they'll be difficult to stop.

The Indian Ocean is perhaps the strangest of the great seas of the world. It is the ancient sea of Zanj to the Arabs who knew it endlessly back into the mists of antiquity. Look on a globe; there, south of Sumatra. Nearly in the center of this immense ocean of mystery lies the tiny dot of Cocos-Keeling Islands. Darwin called it the perfect atoll. It's just a ring of coral reef about eight miles across. There is a cable station on one island, an airstrip on another, and on Home Island live the Clunies-Ross family who manage the group with baronial authority granted by Queen Victoria. The sole industry is the production of copra from the coconut palms which rustle in the cool and pleasant breeze of the steady trade winds.

The schooner *Dirigo II* lies at anchor in the calm lagoon. Her tall spars gleam in the tropic sky as the sun dips near the horizon toward Africa.

Come aboard for dinner. We're having "Duck a la Indian Ocean." The duck cost us six fishhooks from a Malay villager. You will probably pay more.

The duck can be of any size, depending on the company. You

will need one orange, four small onions, ¼ of a lemon, four cloves of garlic, four cloves, one apple, one or two slices of bread, bacon fat, allspice, salt, pepper, and two teaspoons of hot mango chutney.

Wash and wipe the drawn duck inside and out. Rub judgmatically with salt and pepper. Make stuffing by browning two onions and the garlic, all finely chopped, in bacon fat. Add chopped giblets, cube the bread and put into frying pan until lightly browned, stiring diligently. Add a little Wesson oil carefully. Spice with salt, pepper, and allspice. Fill duck and tie it up. Brown duck carefully on all sides in a large pressure cooker.

When brown, mix the chutney with two teaspoons lemon juice and smear over the outside. Stick the cloves into the two remaining onions and place beside duck. Lastly, pop a whole orange in just as it comes from the tree. Put a little water in pressure cooker judging by manufacturer's recommendations; we use about ¾ cup in ours. Cook at ten pounds pressure for about 25 minutes, depending upon the athletics formerly indulged in by the duck.

Chow down! Grub up! When you open the pressure cooker, watch the faces light up as the steam sweeps out.

Some people think this is too short. Good! There'll be more later. And remember, it's not the size of the dog in the fight that counts, but the size of the fight in the dog!

Though not an ocean racer, the Dutch barge yacht has a lot to be said for it—shoal draft, solid comfort, and tabernacled spars.

We bought Ebenhaezer *in Holland and lived aboard there. Then we shipped her to the U.S. (customs called her "an unboxed antique," as she was built in 1893), plopped her into New York Harbor and made our way to Florida for Christmas.*

Her shoal draft and well protected propeller enabled exploration far from the orthodox intracoastal waterway.

Her present owner has cruised the Bahamas with great success.

Ebenhaezer *approaches Zaandam. With a "moped" on deck we had land mobility and the gangplank doubled as a ladder.*

The Cutter Yacht Angantyr

She is named for an ancient Norse king who ruled the Orkney Islands about the time King Arthur sat at the Round Table. In those days the Orkneys were known as the Misty Islands. They still are that, and we thought it would not be too presumptuous to name a vessel of this sort after a king of the Misty Islands. King Angantyr is also mentioned favorably in the Icelandic sagas for his hospitality: "None ever came to the great hall without a warm welcome and food for the belly." A tradition worth emulating.

We have lived aboard this 61' x 17'2" x 5'8" steel, twin-centerboard cutter for more than a year with two small children and a dog. The dog did not cross the Atlantic with us, but the children did.

Launching day was a chilly affair. We had been living in an apartment across the Weser River from Abeking & Rasmussen shipyard in Bremen, Germany, apprehensively watching large islands of ice float downriver. Thankfully, the river didn't freeze over and in she went at high water, January 16, 1964.

We were towed to a fitting-out slip, proving on the way that she was a competent icebreaker. One of the workers, on seeing her plans (drawn by New York designers MacLear & Harris), said, "This isn't a yacht; it's a battle cruiser!"

After noting with considerable relief that she floated just where she should, Horst Lehnert, A. & R.'s general manager, invited us to his house where we applied champagne internally rather than in the usual wasteful fashion. *Skol* and *prosit!*

On the 29th of January, we moved aboard and began to appreciate our diesel-fired heating system. This appreciation was enhanced when we sailed for England on the 6th of February with an inch of snow on deck and great clumps of the stuff falling from the rigging with dismal thuds.

The North Sea lived up to its reputation—cold, rough, steep seas, racing currents, snow squalls, sleet and (as we entered the English Channel and neared the coast) chilling fog. Lots of fun and games. I shall never forget driving through a large part of the North Sea fishing fleet one midwatch with our gloved hands turning blue and sleet needling our faces. There's very little daylight in the latitude of 50° North in this season and this sort of yachting isn't to be recommended except for vessels of *Angantyr's* type and then only after a good deal of experience. The time-honored caveat of eternal vigilance must be well observed.

Horst Lehnert had most kindly loaned us a fine seaman-engineer named Thiemann and Peter Haward's office in England had located a good young sailor, Paul Squire, whose Mayfair manners did not prevent him from being as tough as nails. An A. & R. apprentice, Hans Forster, made a pierhead jump and welcome he was.

How wonderfully the ship behaved! Kindly motion, easy to handle, and surprisingly fast, considering that she is surely the strongest vessel of her size afloat. She balanced like a dream—the twin centerboards giving the hoped-for control of lateral plane. Close-reaching at nine knots, we could stroll away from the wheel for 20 minutes at a time. The balanced rudder gave her one spoke control.

On deck it was cold, but below, the children played in the cozy warmth while the geraniums nodded beside the Madagascar jasmine in the skylight.

With over a ton of freshwater in the double-bottom tanks we took hot baths with luxurious abandon and savory meals came from the gleaming galley with satisfying frequency.

Then down the coast of Merrie England where the names of the ports and headlands ring like ancient bells—North Foreland, Ramsgate, Dover, Dungeness, Selsey Bill. We harbor-hopped quite unashamedly with a careful radio ear on BBC shipping weather reports. Charles Blake, of Camper & Nicholson in Gosport, had offered us a live-aboard winter berth, so on the 24th of February, we stood in through the Solent and entered Portsmouth Harbor. We dipped our ensign as we came abeam of the Royal Navy Signal Station and as the Cross of St. George dropped in reply, we felt that our ship had successfully completed a real shakedown cruise and had come through with flying colors. H.M.S. *Victory* lay to starboard.

We were soon immersed in fitting-out for further adventures. The "Want" and "Do" lists multiplied, were crossed off and grew again. At these times, I comforted myself somewhat wryly with the old saying, "A ship is never finished until she's sunk." Now was the time to correct the "teething troubles" which beset all new vessels. We had surprisingly few of them—a 32-volt alternator was temperamental; the anchor chain was not self-stowing, and so on.

In April, we sailed away with regret from the lovely English spring. Our crew consisted of Captain Robin McClaren, a Seaforth Highlander on leave, Elizabeth Francis, a naval officer's daughter and good sailor, a young English professional, and, of course, my wife Karin, myself, and our two children.

We beat down-Channel in changeable weather until, "Ushant slammed the door on us through the whirling scud alee." Then for the first time, *Angantyr* felt the heave and scend of the Western Ocean. She seemed to like it. Robin's stomach complained for a day or so, but he never missed a watch.

The Bay of Biscay was reasonably kind to us, although I went a mite short of sleep because a large percentage of the world's maritime trade goes by Finisterre and I'm the nervous type of skipper who likes to be on deck in poor visibility and heavy traffic. I certainly appreciated the sea berth Bob Harris designed for me by the chart table.

The days soon grew longer and warmer as we worked our way southward and in a little over a week, we anchored at Las Palmas, Canary Islands. The tropic sun blazed and shorts and protective lotions became the uniform of the day. Liz overdid her sunning, had to stay below for a day, and then began to peel in interestingly mottled patches.

We like the Canaries. The climate is not oppressively tropical and the local people are friendly. Supplies are readily obtainable and reasonably priced.

But the Northeast Trades were humming in the rigging and "the sea was made for sailing"—particularly in these latitudes.

So after five busy days, we weighed anchor and bore off holding well to the south'ard (indeed, passing quite close to the Cape Verdes Islands) which usually affords the fastest passage.

Seventeen peaceful days later, we stood in for Nelson's dockyard, Antigua, British West Indies. On this passage, we simply hung out a moderate-sized reaching jib and guyed the main forward. No pain, no strain, no fancy sails, lots of odd jobs to catch up on; or books to read, or meals to cook and eat. Flying fish were arrowing from the ridged blue sea and Portuguese men-of-war were iridescent in the limpid sunshine. Tropic birds circled the mastheads at dawn and dusk. The track line lengthened across the chart as the noon positions were plotted with the aid of the softly ticking chronometer and my cherished sextant. Then at last, the never-failing thrill of landfall.

Next, "down the islands" to Nassau and Miami. Short stops but lots of fun and fine sailing.

After a brief refit at Bertram's in Miami, we made a direct passage to Newport for the Bermuda Race. Of course, entering *Angantyr* in this event is like entering a percheron in the Kentucky Derby—truer today than a few years ago. Racing has become a highly specialized sport hedged with rules and circulars. Most of the boats called "ocean racers" are not my cup of tea at all, however lively and fun to sail as they may be. The record of gear failures, lost centerboards, steering gear failures and dismastings does not recommend them to this Devout Coward.

Furthermore, the handicapping rule in vogue which rates *Gesture* (a really fine vessel, by the way) as slower than *Angantyr* seems very odd indeed. *Gesture* is our size but five feet narrower, about half the weight, and with 30% more sail area. Either my Physics professor did me dirt or we couldn't possibly be as fast as the lovely *Gesture*. Apparently, the rulemakers (and some of them are friends, I hope!) have no desire to encourage cruising vessels for racing.

Fortunately, I'm blessed with a lot of webfooted friends and when one can make a passage with such people as Junius Beebe, Dick Bertram, Frank MacLear, Sennett Duttenhofer, Bradley Noyes, Bill Lineberger, Wilson Cross, Ray Eaton, Bill Hudgins, and Liz Francis to help with the kids, I don't suppose one could reasonably ask for silver trophies—but, by golly, we got one, anyway. It was presented to us by the crew!

We had a pleasant passage back from Bermuda with two good English types aboard. Then Karin and I harbor-hopped from New England to the Gulf of Mexico with no crew at all except Carita and Eric.

After a year aboard, we have the satisfying feeling that *Angantyr* is exactly as we hoped she would be. As I write, I can hear the children splashing in the bathtub. Karin is starting dinner in the galley and at the moment, as the saying goes, "I wouldn't call the king my cousin!" Our heartfelt thanks go to the designers and builders. We may not fit the racing rules, but I've never known a better cruising machine.

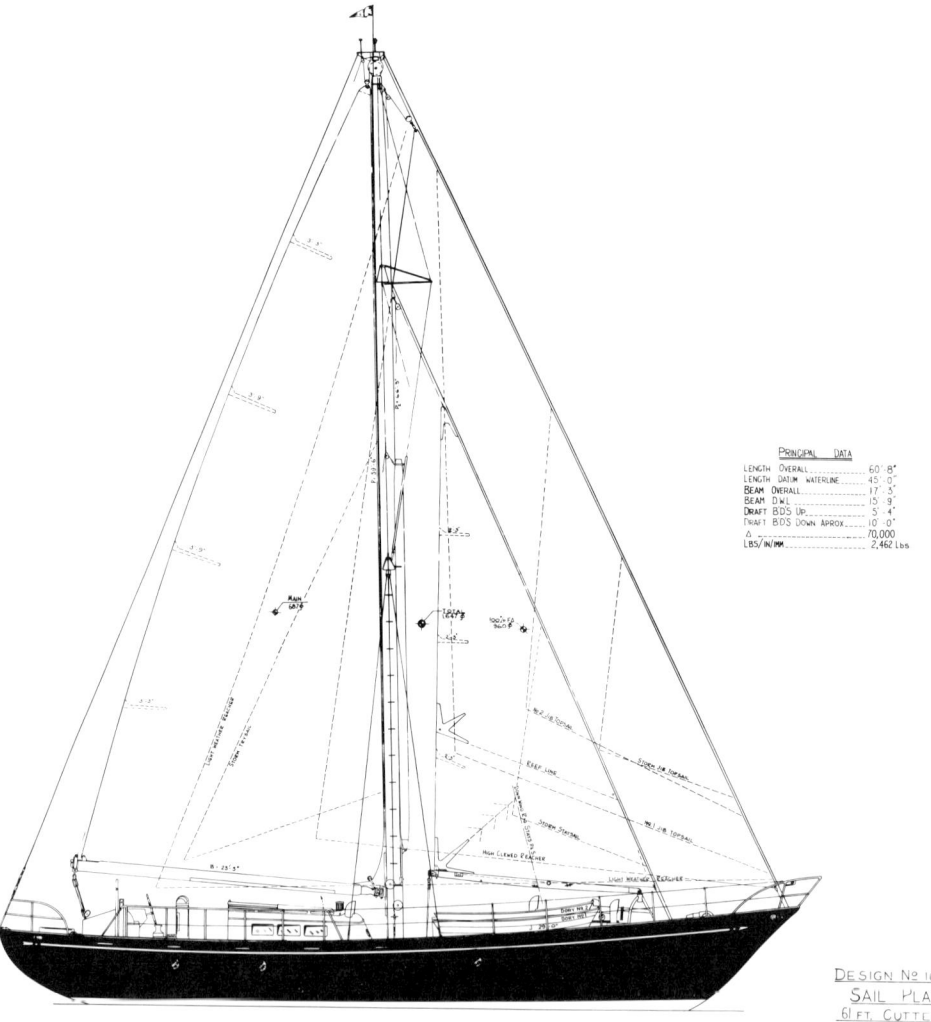

Angantyr began with a letter mailed from Noumea in the South Pacific to Frank MacLear.

Here is her sail plan.

Building commences on the mold-loft floor, but here is the keel itself in the building shed at Abeking and Rasmussen, Lemwerder, West Germany. Photograph by Schroder.

The frame has grown and here the lead ballast is going into the box keel.

"Miss Mercedes" is swung into the completed hull.
The modern diesel engine is worth at least six salty sailormen.

Rudders and rigging are the most common trouble spots on a vessel. The designers were encouraged to make both amply strong on Angantyr.

Launching day. It is cold on the Weser River in January.
Carita is looking over the rail and Karin is holding a booted Eric. Horst Lehnert, Chief Constructor, is accustomed to this sort of thing, but is still emotional about it. I was almost in a state of shock.

We have towed through tinkling ice to the fitting-out float.
The nested dories on deck were designed by Francis Kinney and built by George Luzier.

Cruising in Sweden—the troops go ashore for water at Hellevik.

The gerry cans are filled with sweet well water—Carita, Karin and Eric.

Per dumps the cans of well water into the tank.

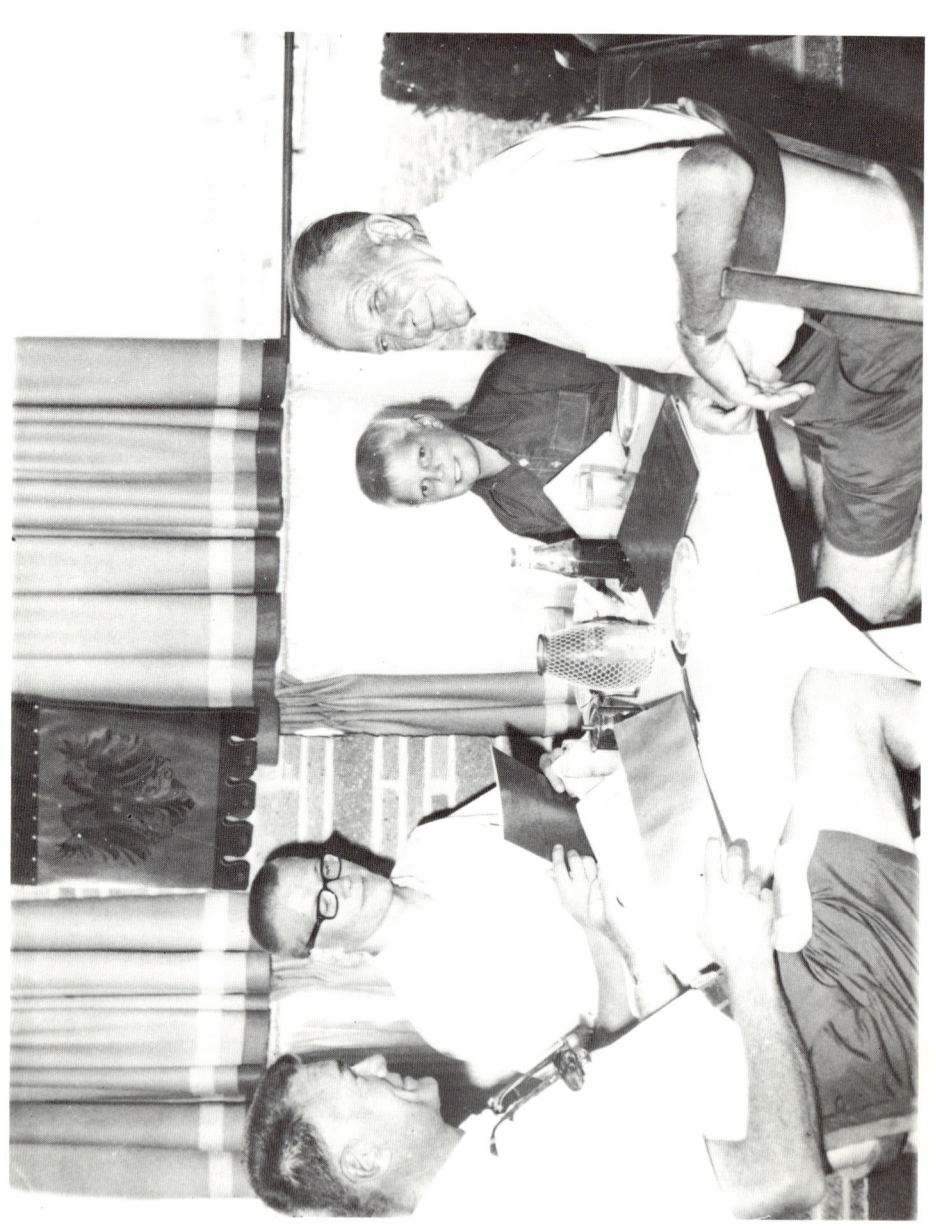

I have made seven Atlantic crossings in Angantyr. *Here is the entire gang having a departure dinner in 1970 in Cape May, New Jersey. We were bound for England. Left to right: J.W. Crawford, Lars Hugoson, my son, Eric, and Henry Davis.*

In the fall of that year I brought the boat back to the West Indies singlehanded via Madeira. It was an interesting and not particularly onerous trip.

Deck view. Lars Hugoson is forward. Both main and roller furling jib are shortened down as we drive for Bishop Rock.

A recent tradewind return from England. Mike Birch is holding the dinner. Rick Stieff is beside him. Harold Hutchinson steers while Ben Brownless looks the happiest.

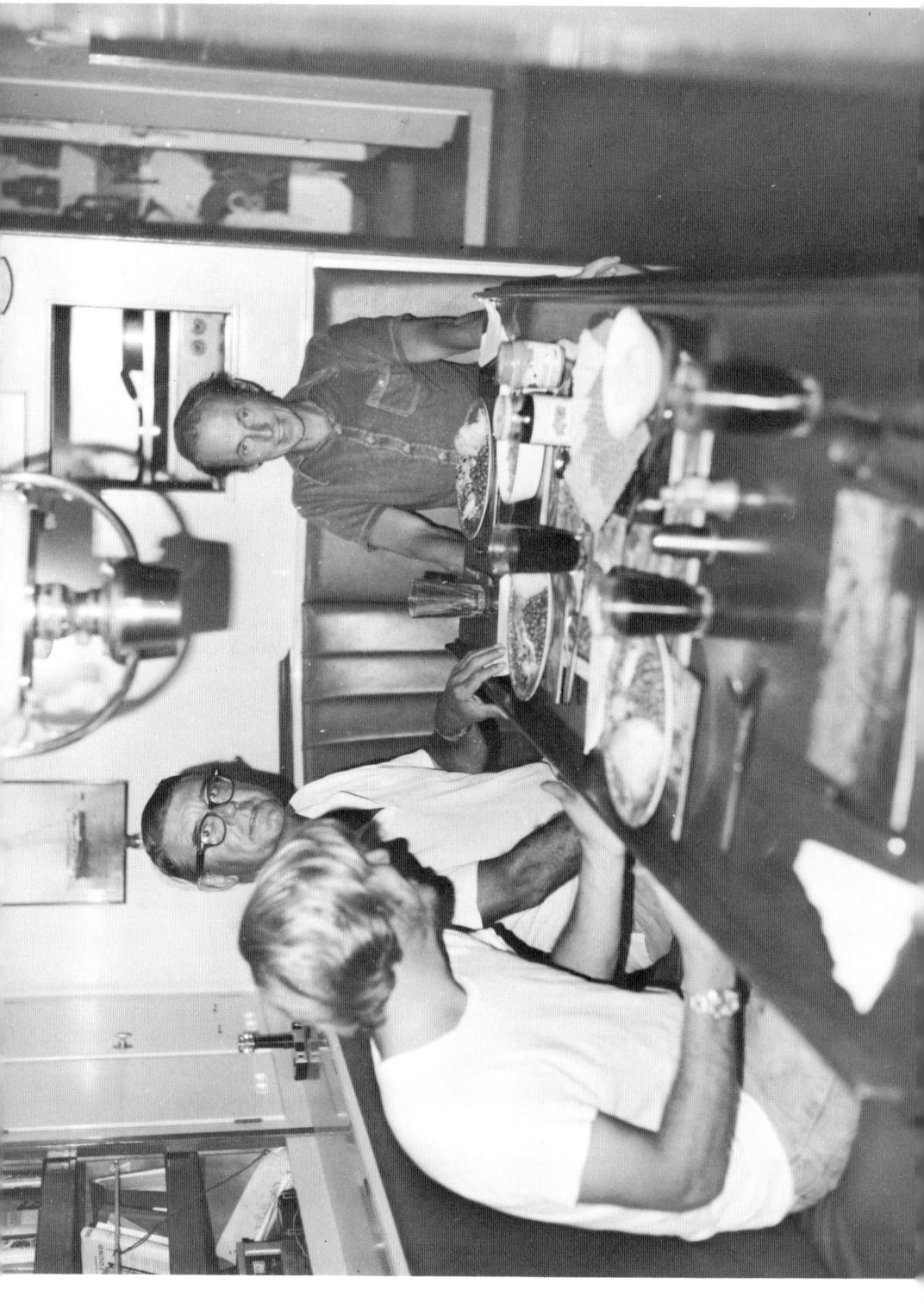

Rick Stieff, left, spins a yarn for Harold Hutchinson and Michael Birch over the gimbaled table.

Angantyr

J.O. Beebe steers with care in the track of the trades and I give you the sailor's farewell; so long!